Sight-Reading for Young Singers

BY EMILY CROCKER

To access audio, visit:
www.halleonard.com/mylibrary

Enter Code
5394-7703-2468-2913

ISBN 978-1-70515-600-1

Visit Hal Leonard Online at
www.halleonard.com

World headquarters, contact:
Hal Leonard
7777 West Bluemound Road
Milwaukee, WI 53213
Email: info@halleonard.com

In Europe, contact:
Hal Leonard Europe Limited
1 Red Place
London, W1K 6PL
Email: info@halleonardeurope.com

In Australia, contact:
Hal Leonard Australia Pty. Ltd.
4 Lentara Court
Cheltenham, Victoria, 3192 Australia
Email: info@halleonard.com.au

INTRODUCTION

Children love to sing and they sing naturally at play as babies, toddlers and up. Children learn songs from their parents, from friends, from media and from school and church. Except in rare circumstances, they do not learn songs from sheet music as instrumentalists might.

Yet, reading music can be an important skill for young singers as they grow into their pre-teen years and can give them advantages in school, in community ensembles, in music theatre groups and in solo singing.

This book is designed to bridge the gap between singing by rote (ear) and reading music. The audio files included will guide the singer through the concepts and the use of solfège (do-re-mi pitch syllables) will give them a framework to begin to connect sound with symbol.

HOW TO USE THIS BOOK

A singer can use this book alone or with a friend, teacher, parent or other adult who can help introduce, practice and master the concepts presented.

There are **no** mistakes! If a particular concept seems difficult, go back to previous songs and exercises and sing them again. Repetition builds confidence.

The audio exercises are included in *My Library* and are organized by chapter. You can either stream the audio or download to your device. Play the audio for each exercise or song, singing the solfège pitch syllables and then the lyrics, repeating each until confident. Concentrate on following the music notation.

The Showcase Solos can be used for motivation and fun and to demonstrate a singer's accomplishment and to reinforce their music reading skills. Use the demo version to read and learn the song and use the backing instrumental track as accompaniment.

ABOUT THE AUTHOR

EMILY HOLT CROCKER taught public school music at all levels for 15 years in Texas. In 1989, she joined Hal Leonard, becoming VP of Choral Publications in 2000, and retiring in 2017 after 29 years. She was founder/director of the Milwaukee Children's Choir from 1994-2009 and named Director Emeritus in 2019 and was founder/director of the Vocal Arts Academy from 2009-2015. As a composer, Ms. Crocker's works have been performed worldwide and she is well known for her work in developing choral and vocal instructional materials. She now resides in Fort Worth, Texas where she composes and is a supporter of the arts.

Chapter One

GIVE ME THE BEAT!

Beat is a steady recurring pulse, like a heartbeat. Tap or clap with a metronome.
You can access demonstration metronome beats on the MyLibrary page,
using the code found on page 1.

BEST DAY OF MY LIFE

Clap the beat and sing the song.

Ooh,   ooh, __ ooh, _____ ooh.

I had a dream so big and loud, I jumped so high, I touched the clouds.

(echo)

Whoa   oh   oh   oh   oh   oh _____

I stretched my hands out to the sky,
We danced with monsters through the night.

(echo)

Whoa   oh   oh   oh   oh   oh _____

I'm never gonna look back, whoa, I'm never gonna give it up, no.
Please don't wake me now. (Two, three, four)

Ooh,   ooh, ___ ooh, _____

This is gonna be the best day of my life,

My   life _____

This is gonna be the best day of my life,

My   life _____

This is gonna be, this is gonna be, this is gonna be the best day of my life.
Everything is looking up, everybody up now.
This is gonna be the best day of my life,

My   life _____

Words and Music by Zachary Barnett, James Adam Shelley, Matthew Sanchez, David Rublin, Shep Goodman and Aaron Accetta

TEMPO

The speed of the beat, faster or slower, is called *tempo*.

Try clapping along with the metronome again.
When you change the metronome setting, you change the tempo.

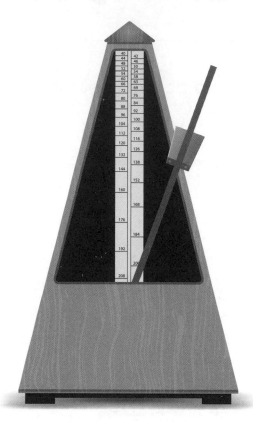

The number stands for "beats per minute" or "bpm."
Try a different tempo and see if you can clap it accurately.

100 bpm	92 bpm
120 bpm	88 bpm
132 bpm	72 bpm
144 bpm	60 bpm

Choose your own tempo!

DON'T WORRY, BE HAPPY

Sing along and clap the beat.

Here's a little song I wrote.
You might want to sing it note for note.

Don't wor-ry, be hap-py.

In every life we have some trouble,
But when you worry you make it double.

Don't wor-ry, be hap-py.

Don't worry, be happy now.

Refrain

Doo doo doo doo doo __ doo doo __ doo doo doo doo

doo doo __ doo doo doo doo doo doo __ doo doo

(sing refrain two times)

By Bobby McFerrin

Ain't got no cash, ain't got no style.
Ain't got no pal to make you smile.

Don't wor-ry,   be hap-py.

When you worry, your face will frown,
And that will bring everybody down.

Don't wor-ry,   be hap-py.

Don't worry, be happy now.

Refrain

Doo   doo doo   doo doo __ doo doo __ doo   doo doo doo

doo doo __ doo doo doo doo   doo doo __ doo doo

(sing refrain four times)

Don't worry, be happy!

MEET THE NOTES

A **note** represents musical sound. The length (duration) of the sound is represented by different note values. Here are three note values:

quarter note   half note   whole note

The following chart represents four beats of sound, with **four quarter notes** having the same duration as **two half notes** or **one whole note**.

The combination of different note values is called **rhythm**.

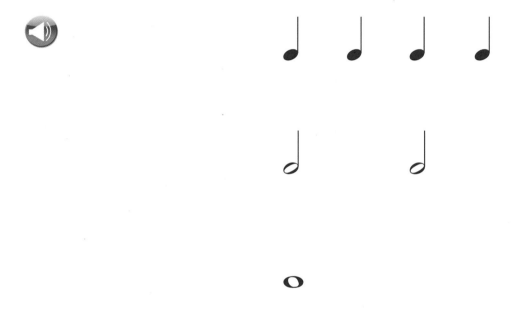

READ QUARTER NOTES

The **quarter note** is commonly assigned the beat. Practice reading **quarter notes** by chanting the syllable "da" while tapping the beat.

da da da da   da da da da   da da da da   da da da da

READ HALF NOTES

A **half note** is two beats of sound. Practice reading **half notes** by chanting the syllables "da-a" while tapping the beat.

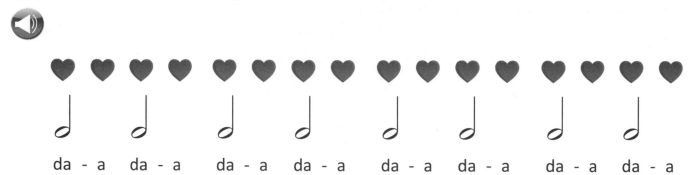

READ WHOLE NOTES

A **whole note** receives four beats of sound. Practice reading **whole notes** by chanting the syllables "da-a-a-a" while tapping the beat.

RHYTHM MIX-UP #1

Now, mix up the note values and read/chant this rhythm pattern.

RHYTHM MIX-UP #2

Read/chant this rhythm pattern. Show the steady beat by tapping.

RHYTHM MIX-UP #3

Read/chant this rhythm pattern. Show the steady beat by tapping.

RAIN, RAIN, GO AWAY

Chant/read the rhythm and tap the steady beat, then sing the song.

Rain, rain, go a - way, come a - gain some oth - er day.

All the chil - dren want to play. Rain, rain, go a - way.

LOVE ME TENDER

Chant/read the rhythm and tap the steady beat, then sing the song.

Love me ten - der, love me sweet; nev - er let me go.

You have made my life com - plete, and I love you so.

Love me ten - der, love me true, all my dreams ful - fill.

For my dar - lin' I love you, and I al - ways will.

MEASURE, METER AND BARLINE

Rhythm can be organized with **barlines** and **measures.** A **barline** is a vertical line that separates rhythm into smaller sections called **measures.**

A **double barline** is placed at the end of a section or piece of music.

Measures and barlines are organized by **meter**. The numbers that identify the meter are called the **time signature** and are placed at the beginning of a song or section of a song.

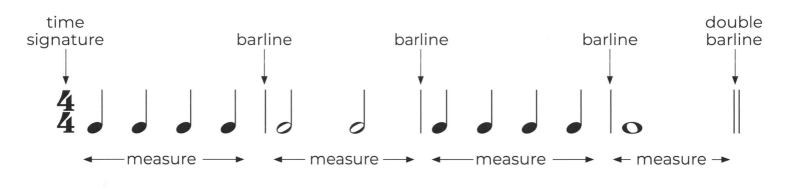

TIME SIGNATURES

Here are three common time signatures:

4 = four beats per measure
4 = quarter note receives the beat

3 = three beats per measure
4 = quarter note receives the beat

2 = two beats per measure
4 = quarter note receives the beat

RHYTHM MIX-UP #4

Identify the meter, then read/chant this rhythm pattern.
Show the steady beat by tapping.

RHYTHM MIX-UP #5

Identify the meter, then read/chant this rhythm pattern.
Show the steady beat by tapping.

RHYTHM MIX-UP #6

Identify the meter, then read/chant this rhythm pattern.
Show the steady beat by tapping.

A-TISKET, A-TASKET

Identify the meter. Chant/read the rhythm and tap the steady beat, then sing the song.

She was truckin' on down the avenue, with not a single thing to do.
She went peck, peck, pecking all around. When she spied it on the ground.

Words and Music by ELLA FITZGERALD and VAN ALEXANDER
© 1938 (Renewed) EMI ROBBINS CATALOG INC.
All Rights Controlled by EMI ROBBINS CATALOG INC. (Publishing) and ALFRED PUBLISHING CO., INC. (Print)
All Rights Reserved Used by Permission

CHAPTER TWO

LET'S MAKE MELODY!

Pitch refers to the highness or lowness of musical sound. Music notes are another name for pitch. Music notes are identified by the first seven letters of the alphabet, from A to G.

The piano keyboard is organized by groups of two and three black keys. The white key to the left of a group of two black keys is always C. The C nearest the middle of the keyboard is called *Middle C*.

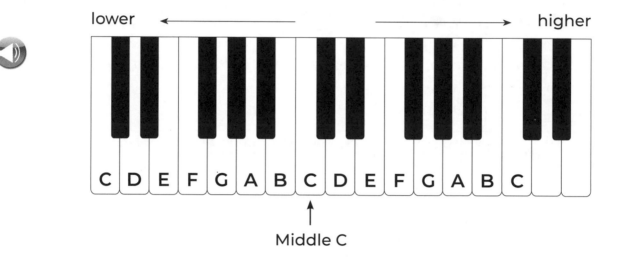

Middle C

Music is written on a staff of five lines and four spaces.

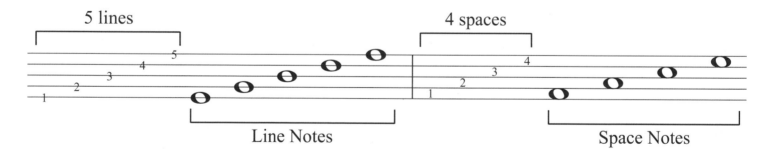

Some notes are written on a line.

line note

Some notes are written on a space.

space note

NOTES ON THE STAFF

The symbol at the beginning of the left side of the staff is called a **treble clef**. Middle C has its own little line below the treble staff called a **ledger** line. Ledger lines can be used below or above a staff.

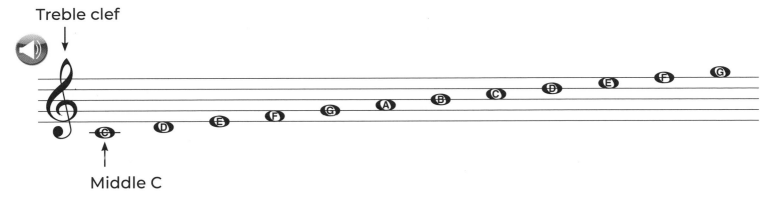

Treble clef

Middle C

A **scale** is a group of pitches lower and higher. Play a scale on a keyboard starting on C and ending on C, using only the white keys and without skipping any keys. This forms a pattern of pitches called a **major scale**.

C Major Scale

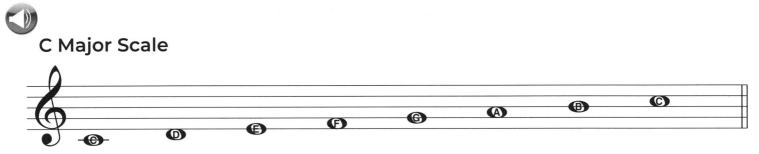

Another way to name pitches is by using **solfège**, a method for singing melodies using Latin note names.

C Major Scale with Solfège

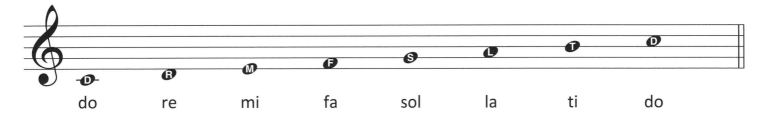

do   re   mi   fa   sol   la   ti   do

🔊 DO-RE-MI
from *The Sound of Music*

Sing this famous song from "The Sound of Music" that uses solfège.

Doe, a deer, a female deer,

Ray, a drop of golden sun.

Me, a name I call myself,

Far, a long, long way to run.

Sew, a needle pulling thread,

La, a note to follow sew.

Tea, a drink with jam and bread,

that will bring us back to do-oh-oh-oh!

Doe, a deer, a female deer,

Ray, a drop of golden sun.

Me, a name I call myself,

Far, a long, long way to run.

Sew, a needle pulling thread,

La, a note to follow sew.

Tea, a drink with jam and bread,

that will bring us back to do!

Do re mi fa sol la ti do sol do!

from THE SOUND OF MUSIC
Lyrics by OSCAR HAMMERSTEIN II
Music by RICHARD RODGERS

ROW, ROW, ROW YOUR BOAT

Sing the lyrics, then sing the solfège.

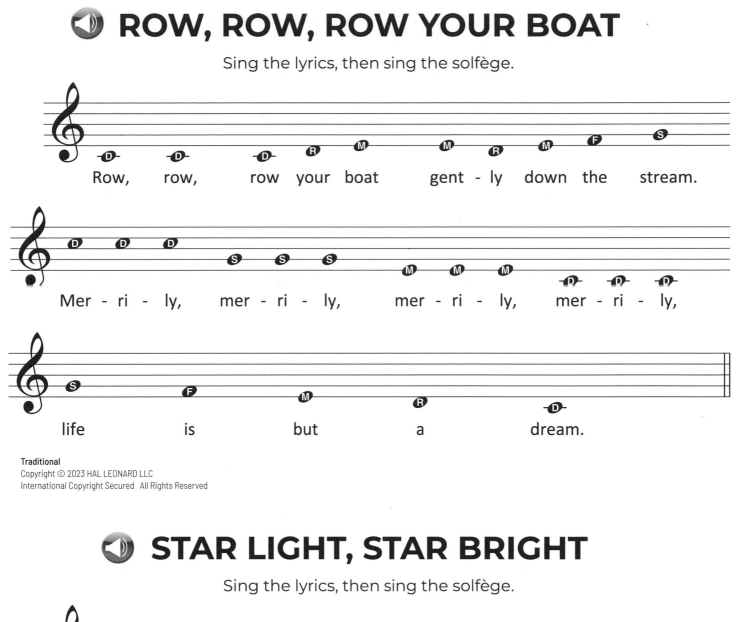

Traditional
Copyright © 2023 HAL LEONARD LLC
International Copyright Secured All Rights Reserved

STAR LIGHT, STAR BRIGHT

Sing the lyrics, then sing the solfège.

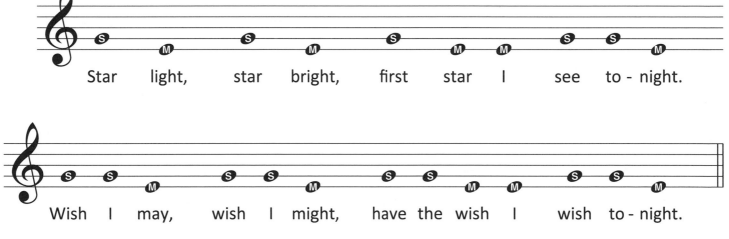

Traditional
Copyright © 2023 HAL LEONARD LLC
International Copyright Secured All Rights Reserved

TWINKLE, TWINKLE LITTLE STAR

Sing the lyrics, then sing the solfège.

Twin - kle,   twin - kle,   lit - tle   star,

How   I   won - der   what   you   are.

Up   a - bove   the   world   so   high,

Like   a   dia - mond   in   the   sky.

Twin - kle,   twin - kle   lit - tle   star,

How   I   won - der   what   you   are.

Traditional
Copyright © 2023 HAL LEONARD LLC
International Copyright Secured All Rights Reserved

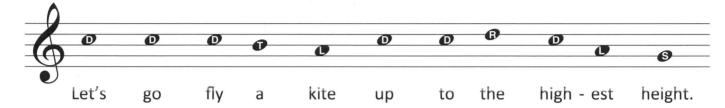

LET'S GO FLY A KITE

1. With tuppence for paper and strings,
you can 'ave your own set of wings.
With your feet on the ground, you're a bird in flight
With your fist 'olding tight
To the string of your kite. Oh, oh, oh,

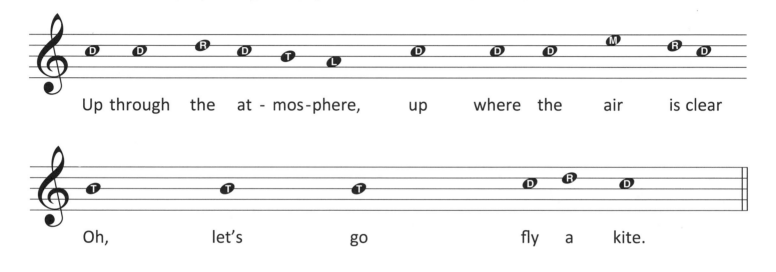

Let's go fly a kite up to the high - est height.

Let's go fly a kit and send it soaring!

Up through the at - mos-phere, up where the air is clear

Oh, let's go fly a kite.

From Walt Disney's MARY POPPINS
Words and Music by RICHARD M. SHERMAN and ROBERT B. SHERMAN
© 1963 Wonderland Music Company, Inc.
Copyright Renewed.
All Rights Reserved.   Used by Permission.

🔊 HOT CROSS BUNS

Traditional
Copyright © 2023 HAL LEONARD LLC
International Copyright Secured All Rights Reserved

🔊 MERRILY WE ROLL ALONG

Traditional
Copyright © 2023 HAL LEONARD LLC
International Copyright Secured All Rights Reserved

🔊 PACHELBEL'S CANON

Traditional
Copyright © 2023 HAL LEONARD LLC
International Copyright Secured All Rights Reserved

🔊 JOYFUL, JOYFUL

Joy - ful, joy - ful, we a - dore thee,

God of glo - ry, Lord of love.

Hearts un - fold like flow'rs be - fore thee

o - p'ning to the sun a - bove.

Melt the clouds of sin and ___ sad - ness,

drive the ___ dark of doubt a - way.

Giv - er of im - mor - tal glad - ness,

fill us with the light of day.

Traditional
Copyright © 2023 HAL LEONARD LLC
International Copyright Secured All Rights Reserved

CHAPTER THREE

MORE ABOUT RHYTHM

In a meter of $\frac{3}{4}$, a dotted half note is held for three beats.
The dot extends the sound by half its value. A dotted half note lasts
as long as a half note plus a quarter note: 3 beats.

TAKE ME OUT TO THE BALL GAME

Sing and tap the steady beat, then sing and clap the rhythm.

Take me out to the ball game. Take me out to the crowd.

Buy me some pea-nuts and crack - er - jack. I don't care if I

nev - er get back. Let me root, root, root for the home team, if

they don't win it's a shame. For it's one, two,

three strikes you're out at the old ball game!

Words by JACK NORWORTH
Music by ALBERT VON TILZER

EDELWEISS

Sing in solfège while tapping the beat. Then, sing in solfège while clapping the rhythm.

Blossom of snow may you bloom and grow,
Bloom and grow forever.

from THE SOUND OF MUSIC
Lyrics by OSCAR HAMMERSTEIN II
Music by RICHARD RODGERS

DIVIDE THE BEAT!

Rhythm is the combination of different note values.

· In $\frac{4}{4}$ meter, a ***quarter note*** receives one beat.

· A ***half note*** receives two beats.

· A ***dotted half note*** receives three beats.

· A ***whole note*** receives four beats.

A quarter note can be divided into two sounds, called ***eighth notes***.

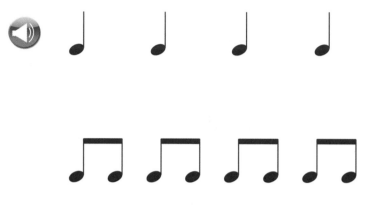

Clap, tap or chant these rhythm exercises that use eighth notes. For quarter, half and whole notes use the syllable "da." For eighth notes, use the syllables "di-di."

TAKE A REST!

A *rest* is silence in music. Rests come in all lengths, just like notes. The beat continues, no matter what type of note or rest value is used.

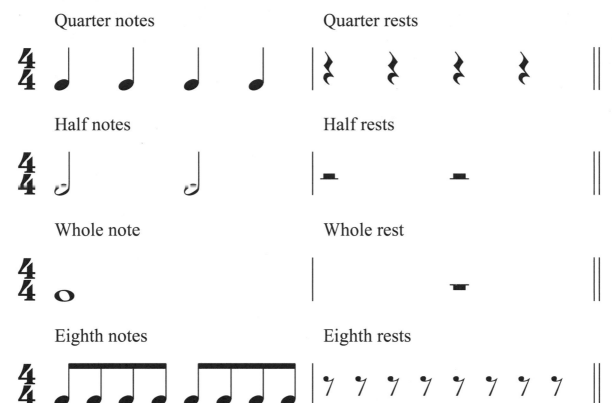

MIX IT UP WITH RESTS

Clap or chant these rhythms using "da-di-di" syllables. For the rests, do a motion with your hands like a shrug.

PEASE PORRIDGE HOT

Read the rhythm on "da-di-di" syllables, then sing in solfège.

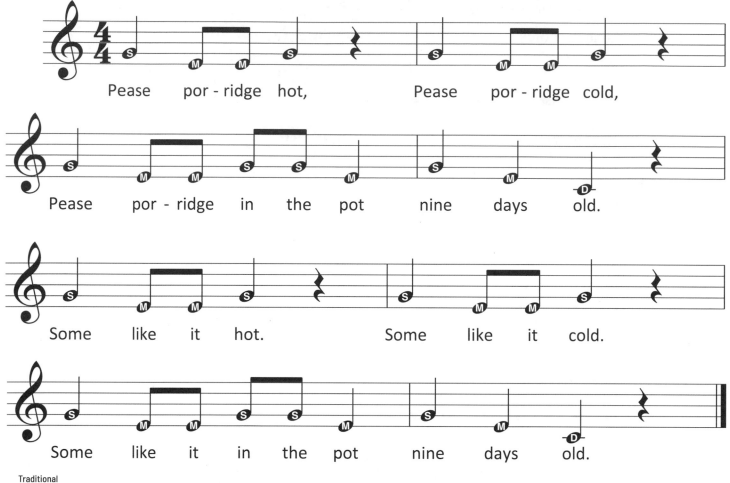

Traditional
Copyright © 2023 HAL LEONARD LLC
International Copyright Secured All Rights Reserved

NAUGHTY KITTY CAT

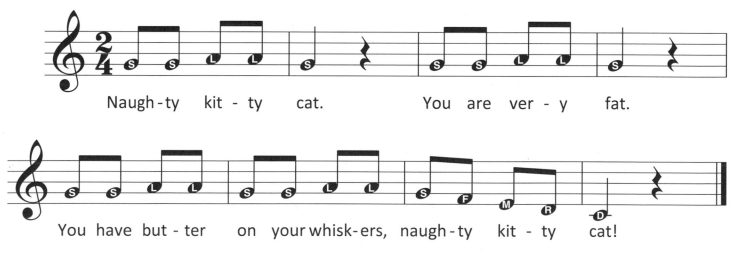

Traditional
Copyright © 2023 HAL LEONARD LLC
International Copyright Secured All Rights Reserved

MELODY MIX-UP

Read the rhythm. Identify the solfège pitches and sing.

FUZZY WUZZY

Fuz - zy Wuz - zy was a bear.

Fuz - zy Wuz - zy had no hair.

Fuz - zy Wuz - zy was - n't fuz - zy was he?

Traditional

HAPPINESS

1. Hap - pi - ness is two kinds of ice cream,
find - ing your skate key, tell - ing the time.

Happiness is learning to whistle,
Tying your shoes for the very first time.
Happiness is playing the drum in your own school band.
And happiness is walking hand in hand.

2. Hap - pi - ness is five dif - f'rent cray - ons,
know-ing a se - cret, climb-ing a tree.

Happiness is finding a nickel,
Catching a firefly, setting him free.
Happiness is being alone ev'ry now and then.
And happiness is coming home again.

From *You're a Good Man, Charlie Brown*
Words and Music by CLARK GESNER
© 1965 JEREMY MUSIC INC.
© Renewed 1993 MPL MUSIC PUBLISHING, INC.

3. Hap-pi-ness   is   morn-ing and eve - ning,   day-time and night-time

too.   For   hap - pi - ness   is   an - y - one,   and

an - y thing   at   all,   that's loved   by   you.

CHAPTER FOUR

A BRAND NEW KEY

F MAJOR

You have been singing songs in the key of C major, based on the C major scale. Songs can also be in other keys.

The **F major scale** starts and ends on F. In this key, you will need to play a **B-flat** to create the correct order of pitches in a major scale.

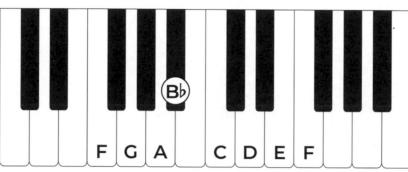

A **flat** (♭) is a symbol that means that the pitch should be changed to the next lower pitch. Another way to show B-flat is to be played is to put a flat on the B line next to the clef sign. This is called a **key signature** and means that all the B notes in the music are to be played as **B-flat**.

Sing the F major scale written on the staff:

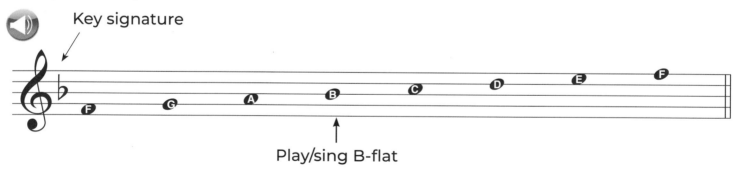

In the new key of F major, F now becomes the key note or "do" and all the solfège syllables shift to the new location.

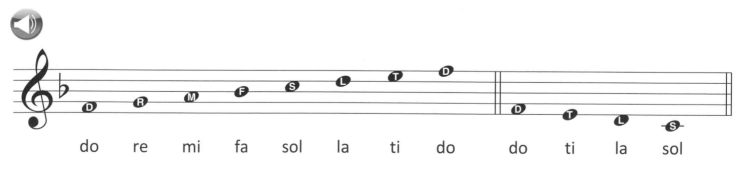

ARE YOU SLEEPING

Are you sleep-ing, are you sleep-ing,

Broth - er John, Broth - er John?

Morn - ing bells are ring - ing, morn - ing bells are ring - ing.

Ding ding dong, ding ding dong.

ROCKY MOUNTAIN

Rock - y moun-tain, rock - y moun-tain, rock - y moun-tain high,

when you're on that rock - y moun-tain, hang your head and cry.

Do, do, do, do, do re - mem - ber me.

Do, do, do, do, do re - mem - ber me.

MELODY MIX-UP

Read or clap the rhythm. Identify the pitch syllables and sing.

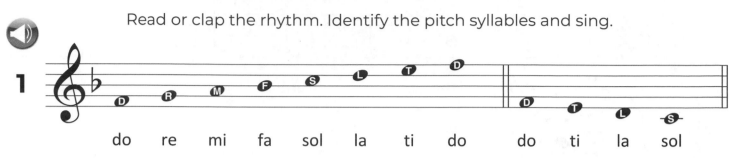

do re mi fa sol la ti do   do ti la sol

SCOTLAND'S BURNING

Clap the rhythm, read and sing the pitch syllables in solfège, then sing the lyrics.

Scot-land's burn-ing, Scot-land's burn-ing! Look out! Look out!
Fire! Fire! Fire! Fire! Pour on wa-ter, pour on wa-ter.

HERE COMES A BLUEBIRD

Here comes a blue-bird fly-ing in my win-dow.
Here comes a blue-bird fly-ing in my win-dow.
Here comes a blue-bird fly-ing in my win-dow.
Oh, won't you come and dance with me.

PART OF YOUR WORLD

Look at this stuff, Isn't it neat?
Wouldn't you think my collection's complete?
Wouldn't you think I'm the girl, the girl who has ev'rything?

Look at this trove, treasures untold.
How many wonders can one cavern hold?
Looking around here you'd think sure, she's got ev'rything.

I've gots gadgets and gizmos aplenty.
I've got whozits and whatzits galore.
You want thingama bobs, I've got twenty.
But who cares? No big deal. I want more.

I wan-na be ___ where the peo-ple are. I wan-na see, ___ wan-na

see 'em danc - in', walk-in' a-round ___ on those, what-d - ya call ___ 'em, oh,

feet. Flip-pin' your fins ___ you don't get too far, ___

Legs are re - quired ___ for jump-in', danc - in', stroll-in' a - long ___ down the,

what's that word a - gain, street. Up where they walk, up where they

From THE LITTLE MERMAID
Music by ALAN MENKEN
Lyrics by HOWARD ASHMAN

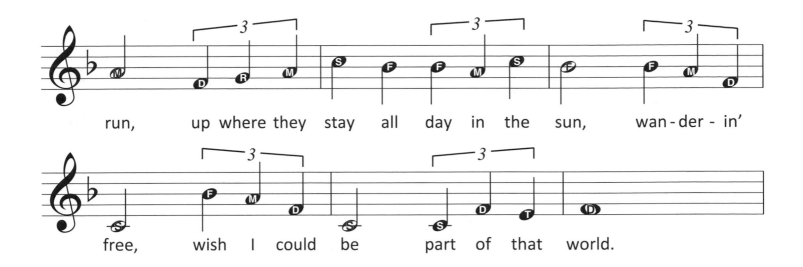

run, up where they stay all day in the sun, wan-der-in'

free, wish I could be part of that world.

What would I give if I could live outta these waters.
What would I pay to spend a day warm on the sand.
Betcha on land they understand.
Bet they don't reprimand their daughters.
Bright young women, sick of swimmin', ready to stand.

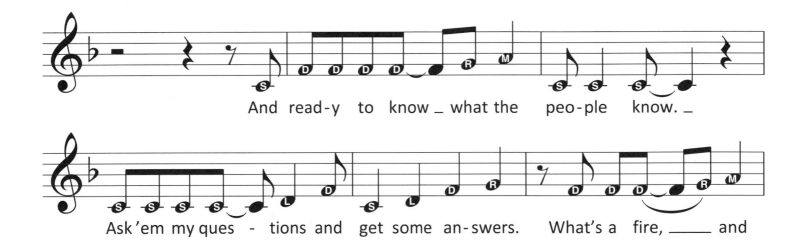

And read-y to know _ what the peo-ple know. _

Ask 'em my ques - tions and get some an-swers. What's a fire, _____ and

why does it, what's the word, burn. When's it my

turn? Would-n't I love, love to ex - plore that shore up a -

bove, _____ out of the sea. Wish I could

be part of that world. _____

CHAPTER 5

MOVING THROUGH THE KEYS

G MAJOR

You have sung songs in the key of **C major** and the key of **F major**. Songs can be any key, including **G major.**

The **G major scale** starts and ends on G. In this key you will need an **F-sharp** to create the correct order of pitches in a major scale.

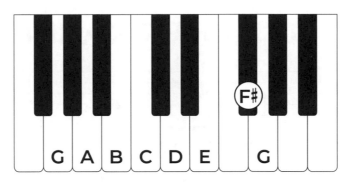

A **sharp** # is a symbol that means that the pitch should be changed to the next higher pitch. Another way to show that F-sharp is to be played is to put a sharp on the F line next to the clef sign. This is called a **key signature** and means that all the F notes in the music are to be played as **F-sharp**.

Sing the G major scale written on the staff:

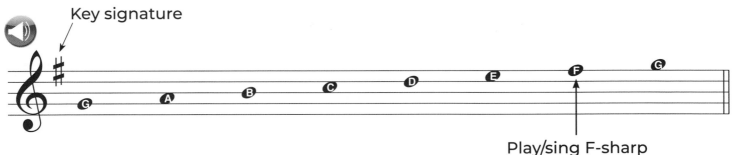

In the new key of G major, G now becomes the keynote or "do" and all the solfège syllables shift to the new location.

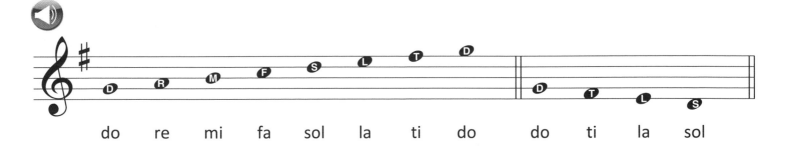

| do | re | mi | fa | sol | la | ti | do | do | ti | la | sol |

FAIS DO-DO

Clap the rhythm, sing the solfège pitches, then sing the lyrics.

Fais do - do and let us go dream - ing.

Fais do - do, come dream - ing with me.

OLD MISTER RABBIT

Old Mis - ter Rab - bit, you got a might - y hab - it of

sneak - ing in my gar - den and eat - ing up my cab - bage.

FROG IN THE MEADOW

Frog in the mead - ow, can't get him out.

Take a lit - tle stick and stir him a - bout.

Hide frog! Run a - way! Come back an - oth - er day.

MELODY MIX-UP

Clap the rhythm, identify the pitch syllables, then sing the melody in solfège.

1

do   re   mi   fa   sol   la   ti   do   do   ti   la   sol

2

3

4

🔊 I'M GONNA SING

Clap the rhythm, then sing the pitch syllables in solfège, then sing the lyrics.

I'm gon - na sing when the spir - it says

"Sing." I'm gon - na sing when the spir - it says

"Sing." ___ I'm gon - na sing when the spir - it says

"Sing." And o - bey the spir - it of the Lord.

🔊 MARY ANN

All day, all night, Miss Mar - y Ann, ___

down by the sea - side sift - ing sand. _

E - ven lit - tle chil - dren love Mar - y Ann, ___

down by the sea - side sift - ing sand. _

WHAT A WONDERFUL WORLD

I see trees of green, red ros - es, too;
I see them bloom for me and you, and I
think ___ to my-self, "What a won - der - ful world."
I see skies of blue and clouds of white, the
bright ___ bless-ed day, the dark ___ sa - cred night and I
think __ to my-self, "What a won - der-ful world."

The colors of the rainbow, so pretty in the sky,
Are also on the faces of people goin' by.
I see friends shakin' hands, sayin', "How do you do!"
They're really sayin', "I love you."

Words and Music by GEORGE DAVID WEISS and BOB THIELE

I hear ba - bies cry, I watch them grow;

they'll learn much more than I'll _____ ev - er know, and I

think to my-self, "What a won-der-ful world." Yes, I

think to my-self, "What a won-der-ful world."

Chapter Six

FOUR SOUNDS ON THE BEAT

Rhythm is the combination of different note values.

- In ♩ meter, a *quarter note* receives one beat.

- A *half note* receives two beats.

- A *dotted half note* receives three beats.

- A *whole note* receives four beats.

A quarter note can be divided into two sounds, called *eighth notes*.
A quarter note may also be divided into four sounds, called *sixteenth notes*.

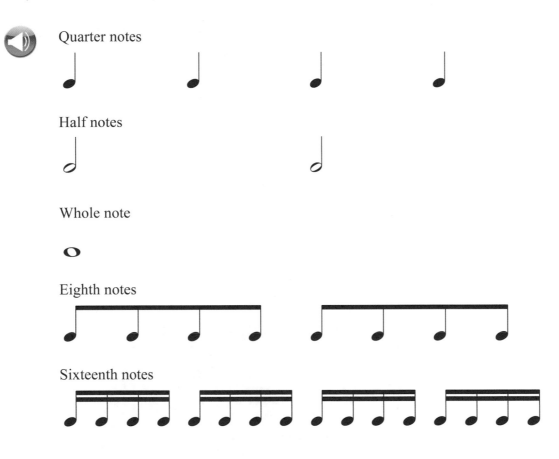

Quarter notes

Half notes

Whole note

Eighth notes

Sixteenth notes

READ SIXTEENTH NOTES

Sixteenth notes can be played and sung in groups of four. Sixteenth notes can be combined with eighth notes. Keep a steady beat and read these rhythms.

🔊 HUCKLEBERRY PIE

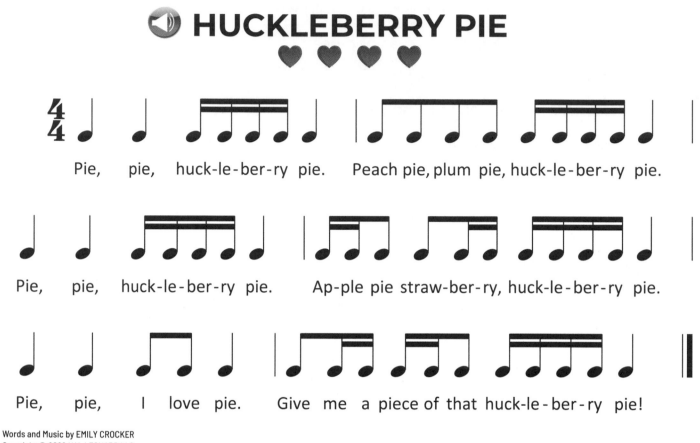

Pie, pie, huck-le-ber-ry pie. Peach pie, plum pie, huck-le-ber-ry pie.

Pie, pie, huck-le-ber-ry pie. Ap-ple pie straw-ber-ry, huck-le-ber-ry pie.

Pie, pie, I love pie. Give me a piece of that huck-le-ber-ry pie!

Words and Music by EMILY CROCKER
Copyright © 2022 HAL LEONARD LLC
All Rights Reserved International Copyright Secured

ANIMAL RHYTHMS

4/4 Al - li - ga - tor, ban - di - coot, cock - a - too, dove.

Ea - gle, fox, grass-hop-per, hawk. Inch worm, jel - ly- fish, kang-a - roo, loon.

Moose, night-crawl-er, os - trich, pig. Queen-snake, rab - bit, sal - a-man-der, tick.

Ur - chin, vi-per-fish wal-la- by, xe - nops, Yak! Ze - bra! How a-bout that!

Words and Music by EMILY CROCKER
Copyright © 2022 HAL LEONARD LLC
All Rights Reserved International Copyright Secured

SING SIXTEENTH NOTES

Clap the rhythm, sing the solfège pitches and sing the lyrics. What key are you in?

🔊 LOVE SOMEBODY

🔊 THE PAW PAW PATCH

MELODY MIX-UP

Clap the rhythm. Identify the pitches and sing in solfège.

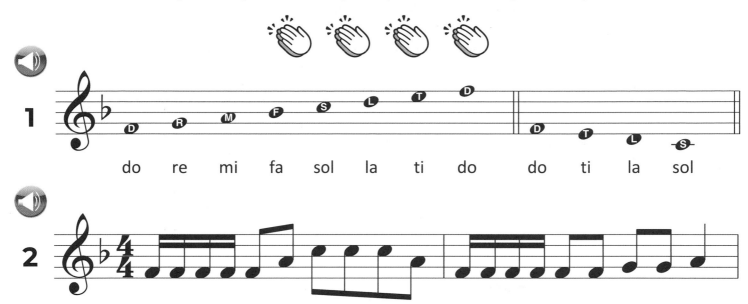

do   re   mi   fa   sol   la   ti   do   do   ti   la   sol

🔊 BLACKBIRD

REVIEW: A flat ♭ is a symbol that means that the pitch should be changed to the next lower pitch. When you have a flat that is not in the key signature, it is called an ***accidental*** and means that the flat only changes the pitches in the measure where it appears. Find the accidentals in this song. Also notice that the meter changes within this song. Keep track of the rhythm especially when you have rests.

Words and Music by JOHN LENNON and PAUL McCARTNEY

Copyright © 1968, 1969 Sony/ATV Publishing LLC
All Rights Administered by Sony/ATV Music Publishing LLC, 424 Church Street, Suite 1200, Nashville, TN 37219
International Copyright Secured All Rights Reserved

Black - bird sing - ing in the dead of night,

take these sunk-en eyes and learn to see;

all your life _____ you were on - ly wait-ing for this

mo-ment to be free. Black - bird, fly, black - bird,

fly in - to the light of a dark black _ night.

Black - bird,

fly, black - bird, fly in - to the

light of a dark black _ night.

Black-bird sing-ing in the dead of night, take these bro-ken wings and learn to fly; all your life _____ you were on - ly wait-ing for this mo-ment to a - rise.

You were on - ly wait-ing for this mo-ment to a - rise.

CHAPTER SEVEN

IN A MINOR MOOD

A **scale** is a group of pitches lower and higher. In addition to **major scales** like C major, F major and G major, there are other types of scales.

Play a scale on a keyboard starting on A and ending on A, using only the white keys and without skipping any keys. This forms a pattern of pitches called a **minor scale**.

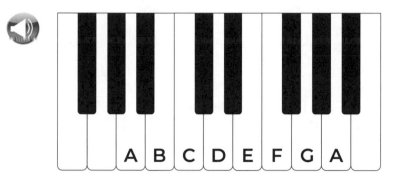

Sing the **A minor scale** using the letter names.

A Minor Scale

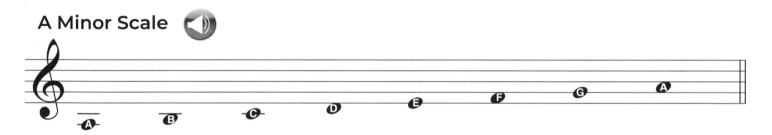

Sing the **A minor scale** in solfège. Notice that the minor scale starts and ends on la.

A Minor Scale in Solfège

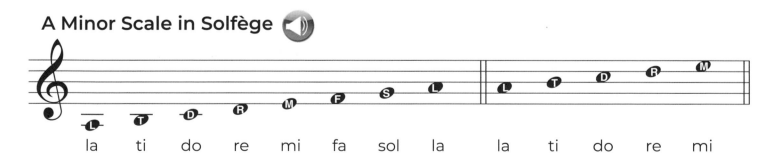

la ti do re mi fa sol la la ti do re mi

SONGS IN MINOR

Clap the rhythm, then sing the solfège and lyrics.

🔊 AH POOR BIRD

🔊 OLD ABRAM BROWN

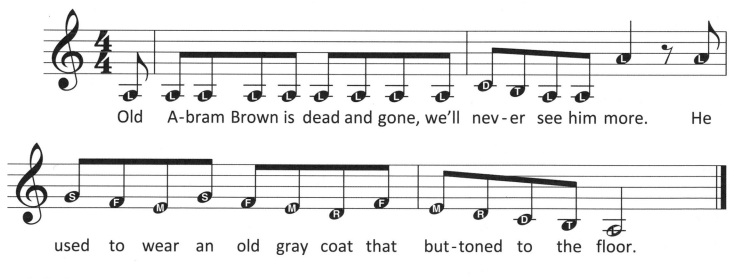

MELODY MIX-UP

Clap the rhythm. Identify the pitch syllables and sing.

A Minor Scale in Solfège

la ti do re mi fa sol la   la ti do re mi

CASTLE ON A CLOUD

Things to notice: This song uses an uneven rhythm of **dotted eighth-sixteenth** and **sixteenth rests**. As you listen to the recording notice how the rhythm sounds.

There are several **accidentals** in this song. Find them and notice how the pitch is changed.

There is a cas - tle on a cloud.

I like to go there in my sleep.

Aren't an - y floors for me to sweep,

not in my cas - tle on a cloud.

from LES MISÉRABLES
Music by CLAUDE-MICHEL SCHÖNBERG
Lyrics by Alain Boublil, JEAN-MARC NATEL and HERBERT KRETZMER
Music and French Lyrics Copyright © 1980 by Editions Musicales Alain Boublil
English Lyrics Copyright © 1986 by Alain Boublil Music Ltd. (ASCAP)
Mechanical and Publication Rights for the U.S.A. Administered by Alain Boublil Music Ltd. (ASCAP) c/o Spielman Koenigsberg & Parker, LLP, Richard Koenigsberg, 1675 Broadway, 20th Floor, New York, NY 10019, Tel 212-453-2500, Fax 212-453-2550, ABML@skpny.com
International Copyright Secured. All Rights Reserved. This music is copyright. Photocopying is illegal.
All Performance Rights Restricted.

There is a room that's full of toys.

There are a hun - dred boys and girls.

No - bod - y shouts or talks too loud,

not in my cas - tle on a cloud.

There is a la - dy all in white, _ holds me and sings a lull - a - by. She's

nice to see and she's soft to touch. She says, "Co-sette, I love you ver - y much."

I know a place where no one's lost.

I know a place where no one cries.

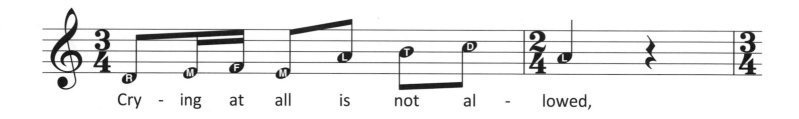

Cry - ing at all is not al - lowed,

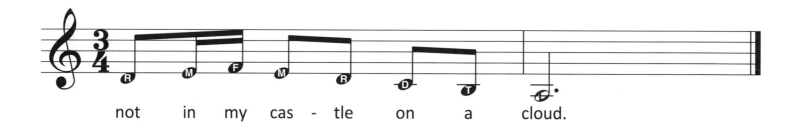

not in my cas - tle on a cloud.

SONGS IN E MINOR

Minor scales can start on any pitch. The **E minor scale** starts and ends on E and needs an F-sharp to create the correct order of pitches for a minor scale.

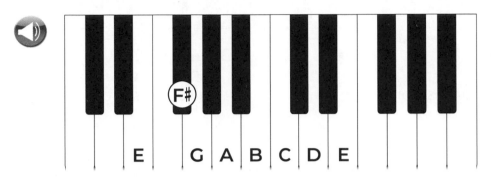

Play or sing the E minor scale in solfège.

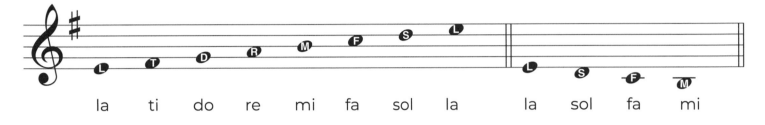

la   ti   do   re   mi   fa   sol   la   la   sol   fa   mi

🔊 SHALOM CHAVERIM

Sha - lom cha-ve-rim, sha - lom cha-ve-rim, sha -

lom, sha - lom. Till we meet a-gain, till

we meet a-gain, sha - lom, sha - lom.

Traditional
Copyright © 2023 HAL LEONARD LLC
All Rights Reserved International Copyright Secured

MY FAVORITE THINGS

Clap the rhythm. Read the pitches in solfège (notice the accidentals). Sing the lyrics.

from THE SOUND OF MUSIC
Lyrics by OSCAR HAMMERSTEIN II
Music by RICHARD RODGERS

door - bells and sleigh - bells and schnitz - el with noo - dles,

wild geese that fly with the moon on their wings,

2

these are a few of my fa - vor - ite things.

Girls in white dress - es with blue sat - in sash - es,

snow - flakes that stay on my nose and eye - lash - es,

sil - ver white win - ters that melt in - to springs,

these are a few of my fa - vor - ite things.

When the dog bites, when the bee stings,

when I'm feel - ing sad, _____ I

sim - ply re - mem - ber my fa - vor - ite things and

then I don't feel so

1.
bad.

2.
bad. _____

CHAPTER EIGHT

SING AROUND THE KEYS

Music can be written in many different keys and sometimes not in any key at all. Here is a chart of major and minor key signatures. When you learn a new song, identify the key signature and the pitch syllables for that song in solfège.

MAJOR KEYS

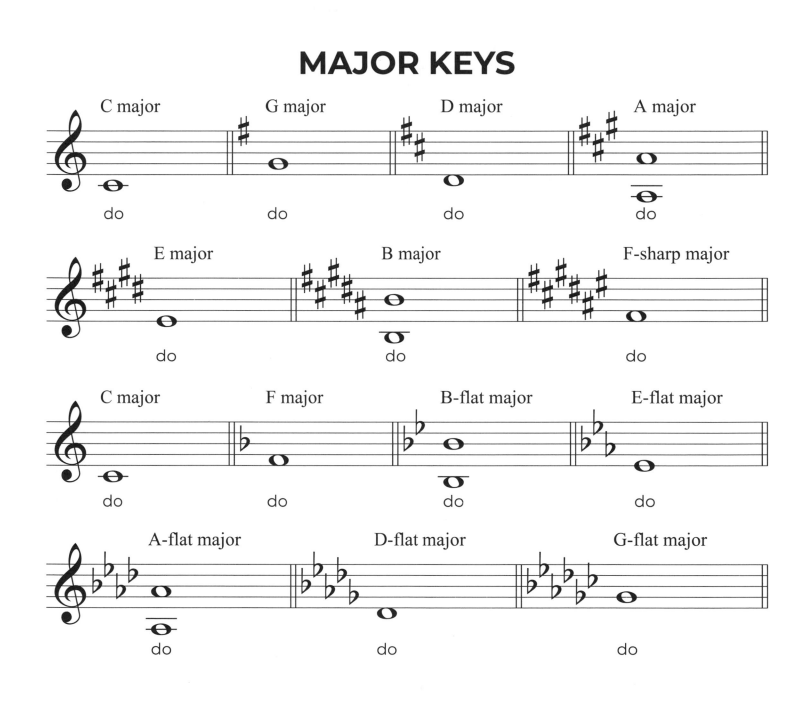

MINOR KEYS

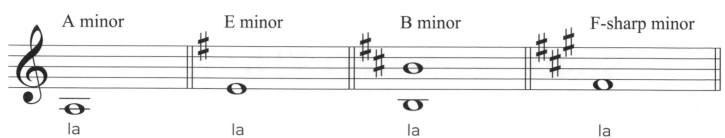

A minor   E minor   B minor   F-sharp minor

la   la   la   la

C-sharp minor   G-sharp minor   D-sharp minor

la   la   la

A minor   D minor   G minor   C minor

la   la   la   la

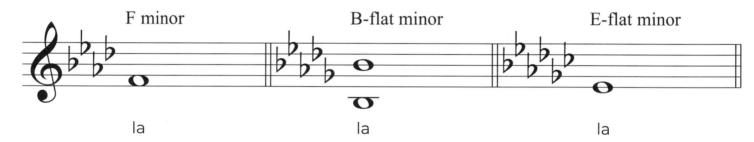

F minor   B-flat minor   E-flat minor

la   la   la

KUMBAYA

Identify the key of the song and write the scale on the staff beginning with *do*.

Kum - ba - ya, my Lord, _____ kum - ba - ya.

Kum - ba - ya, my Lord, _____ kum - ba - ya.

Kum - ba - ya, my Lord, _____ kum - ba - ya.

Oh, Lord, _____ kum - ba - ya.

🔊 MAKE NEW FRIENDS

Identify the key of the song and write the scale on the staff beginning with *do*.
Clap the rhythm, identify the pitches, sing in solfège, then sing the lyrics.

Make new friends, but keep ___ the ___ old. ___

One is sil - ver and the oth - er gold.

🔊 MICHAEL, ROW THE BOAT ASHORE

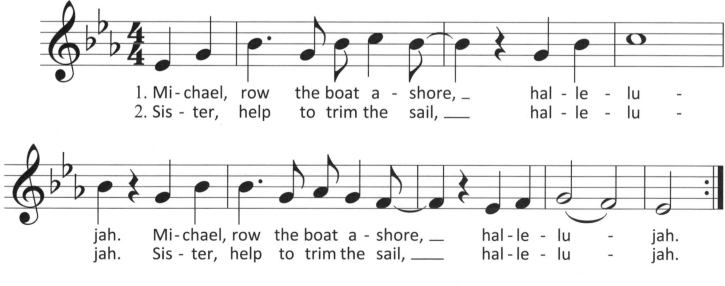

1. Mi - chael, row the boat a - shore, _ hal - le - lu -
2. Sis - ter, help   to trim the sail, ___ hal - le - lu -

jah. Mi - chael, row the boat a - shore, _ hal - le - lu - jah.
jah. Sis - ter, help to trim the sail, ___ hal - le - lu - jah.

3. Jordan river is deep and wide, hallelujah.
Milk and honey on the other side, hallelujah.

🔊 LOVE IS AN OPEN DOOR

ACCIDENTALS: Notice the *natural* symbols in this song. These are *accidentals* that cancel a sharp or flat.

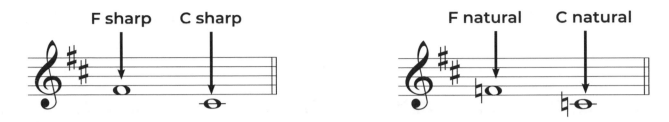

F sharp   C sharp   F natural   C natural

Identify the key of the song and write the scale on the staff beginning with **do**. Clap the rhythm, identify the pitches, sing in solfège, then sing the lyrics. Also notice the song *changes keys* from D major to E major. All the solfège pitches shift to the new location.

All my life has been a se - ries of doors ___ ___ in my face, ___ and then sud-den-ly I bump in-to you! ___

I've been search-ing my whole life to find my own place. ___ And may-be it's the par - ty talk - ing or the cho-c'late fon - due. But with you,

from FROZEN
Music and Lyrics by Kristen Anderson-Lopez and Robert Lopez
© 2013 Wonderland Music Company, Inc.
All Rights Reserved. Used by Permission.

but with you, __ I found my place, I see your face, and it's

noth-ing like __ I've ev-er known __ be - fore. Love is an o - pen

door. _____ Love is an o - pen door! _____

_____ Love is an o - pen door with you, __ with you, with

you, with you. Love is an o - pen door.

I mean it's cra - zy. We fin-ish each oth-er's

sand-wich-es.   I nev-er met some-one who thinks so much _ like

me.   Our men-tal syn - chro-ni-za - tion   can

have but one __ ex-pla-na-tion: You and I _____ were just meant to be. _

____   Say good - bye _____ to the pain _

____ of the past. _   We don't have to feel it an - y - more. _

____   Love is an o - pen door. _____

Love is an o - pen door. _____

_____ Life can be so ___ much more with you, _ with you, with

you, with you. Love is an o - pen door.

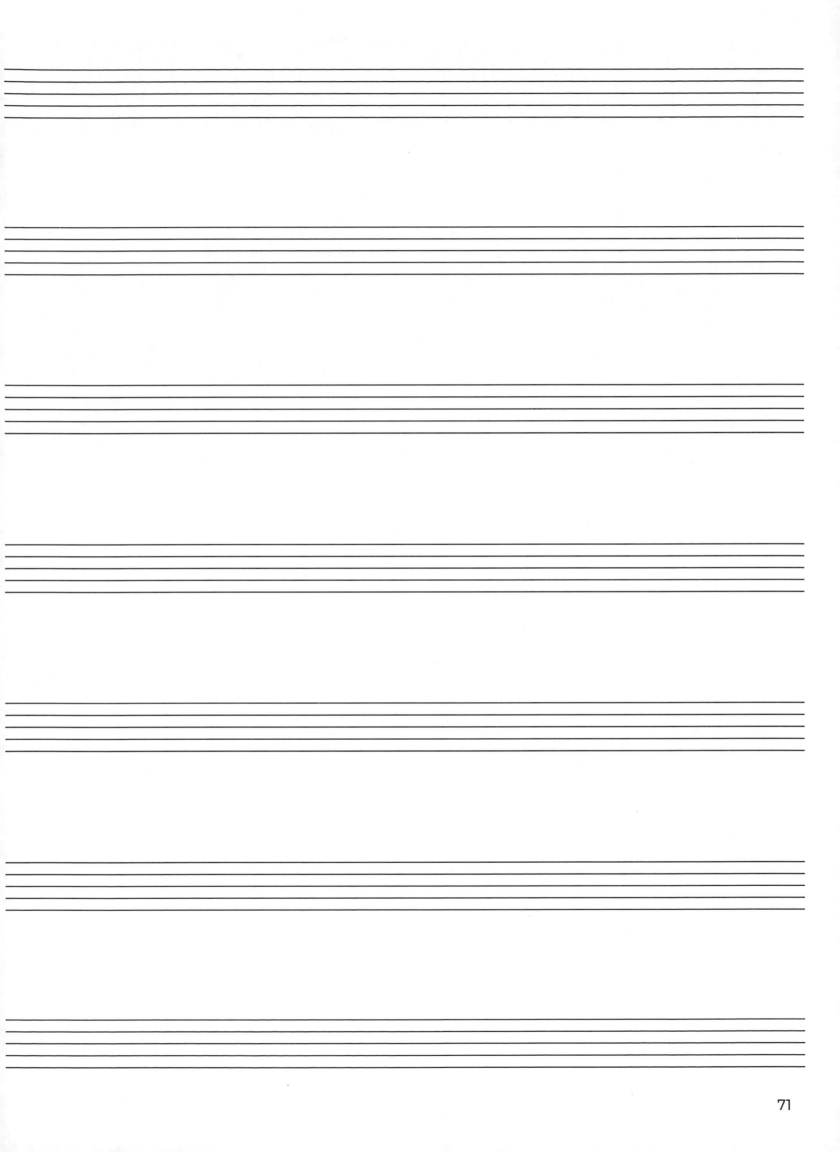

HAL LEONARD METHODS FOR KIDS

This popular series of method books for youngsters provides accessible courses that teach children to play their instrument of choice faster than ever before. The clean, simple page layouts ensure kids' attention remains on each new concept. Every new song presented builds on concepts they have learned in previous songs, so kids stay motivated and progress with confidence. These methods can be used in combination with a teacher or parent. The price of each book includes access to audio play-along and demonstration tracks online for download or streaming.

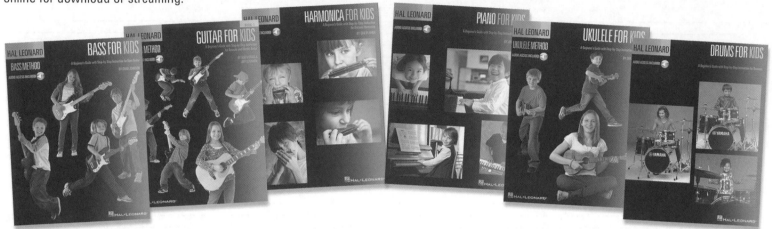

GUITAR FOR KIDS, METHOD BOOK 1
by Bob Morris and Jeff Schroedl

This method is equally suitable for students using electric or acoustic guitars. It features popular songs, including: Hokey Pokey • Hound Dog • I'm a Believer • Surfin' USA • This Land Is Your Land • Yellow Submarine • and more.
00865003 Book/Online Audio.............................$14.99

GUITAR FOR KIDS, METHOD BOOK 2
by Chad Johnson

Equally suitable for children using electric or acoustic guitars, this book picks up where Book 1 left off. Songs include: Dust in the Wind • Eight Days a Week • Fields of Gold • Let It Go • Oye Como Va • Rock Around the Clock • and more.
00128437 Book/Online Audio.............................$14.99

GUITAR FOR KIDS: BLUES METHOD BOOK
by Dave Rubin

Cool blues riffs, chords and solos are featured in this method, which is suitable for children using electric or acoustic guitars. Lessons include: selecting your guitar • parts of the guitar • holding the guitar • hand position • easy tablature • strumming & picking • blues riffs & chords • basic blues soloing • and more.
00248636 Book/Online Audio.............................$14.99

GUITAR FOR KIDS SONGBOOK

This supplement follows chords in the order they are taught in book 1 of the guitar method. 10 songs: At the Hop • Don't Worry, Be Happy • Electric Avenue • Every Breath You Take • Feelin' Alright • Fly like an Eagle • Jambalaya (On the Bayou) • Love Me Do • Paperback Writer • Three Little Birds.
00697402 Book/Online Audio.............................$12.99

GUITAR FOR KIDS METHOD & SONGBOOK

00697403 Book/Online Audio.............................$22.99

Prices, contents, and availability subject to change without notice.

BASS FOR KIDS METHOD BOOK
by Chad Johnson

Topics in this method book include selecting a bass, holding the bass, hand position, reading music notation and counting, and more. It also features popular songs including: Crazy Train • Every Breath You Take • A Hard Day's Night • Wild Thing • and more. Includes tab.
00696449 Book/Online Audio.............................$14.99

DRUMS FOR KIDS METHOD BOOK

Topics included in this method book for young beginning drummers include setting up the drumset, music reading, learning rhthms, coordination, and more. Includes the songs: Another One Bites the Dust • Crazy Train • Free Fallin' • Living After Midnight • Old Time Rock & Roll • Stir It Up • When the Levee Breaks • and more.
00113420 Book/Online Audio.............................$14.99

HARMONICA FOR KIDS METHOD BOOK
by Eric Plahna

Lessons include topics such as hand position, basic chord playing, learning melodies, and much more. Includes over 30 songs: All My Loving • Happy Birthday to You • Jingle Bells • Over the River and Through the Woods • Scarborough Fair • Take Me Out to the Ball Game • This Land Is Your Land • You Are My Sunshine • and more.
00131101 Book/Online Audio.............................$14.99

PIANO FOR KIDS METHOD BOOK
by Jennifer Linn

This fun, easy course incorporates popular songs including: Beauty and the Beast • Heart and Soul • Let It Go • Over the Rainbow • We Will Rock You • and more classical/folk tunes. Topics covered include parts of the piano, good posture and hand position, note reading, dynamics and more.
00156774 Book/Online Audio.............................$13.99

HAL•LEONARD®
www.halleonard.com

PIANO FOR KIDS SONGBOOK
by Jennifer Linn

A supplementary companion to the method book for piano, this book presents classic songs and contemporary hits which progress in like manner with the method book. Includes: All of Me • Can't Stop the Feeling • Do Re Mi • Linus and Lucy • and more.
00217215 Book/Online Audio.............................$12.99

PIANO FOR KIDS CHRISTMAS SONGBOOK
by Jennifer Linn

Includes: Go, Tell It on the Mountain • I Want a Hippopotamus for Christmas • Jingle Bell Rock • Jingle Bells • Mary, Did You Know? • Rudolph the Red-Nosed Reindeer • Up on the Housetop • We Three Kings of Orient Are • and more.
00238915 Book/Online Audio.............................$12.99

UKULELE FOR KIDS
by Chad Johnson

This book features popular songs including: Barbara Ann • The Hokey Pokey • Rock Around the Clock • This Land Is Your Land • Yellow Submarine • You Are My Sunshine • and more. Lessons include: selecting your uke; parts of the uke; holding the uke; hand position; reading music notation and counting; notes on the strings; strumming and picking; and more!
00696468 Book/Online Audio.............................$14.99

UKULELE FOR KIDS SONGBOOK

Strum your favorite hits from Jason Mraz, Disney, U2 and more! This collection can be used on its own, as a supplement to the *Ukulele for Kids* method book or any other beginning ukulele method. Songs: Don't Worry, Be Happy • I'm Yours • The Lion Sleeps Tonight • Riptide • The Siamese Cat Song • and more.
00153137 Book/Online Audio.............................$12.99

UKULELE FOR KIDS METHOD & SONGBOOK
00244855 Book/Online Audio.............................$22.99